BAD PENNY

A John Treehorn Mystery
Short Read #1

DINAH MILLER

ISBN 978-0-9979826-6-4

BAD PENNY A John Treehorn Mystery – Short Read #1 is a work of fiction. Names, characters, places, and incidents are either the product of the author's vivid imagination or are used fictitiously. Any resemblance to actual persons, living or dead, events, or locales is entirely coincidental.

Published by:
New York Productions, LLC
P. O. Box 175
Churubusco, NY 12923

Printed in the United States of America

Cover Artwork by Leonie Cheetham
https://www.facebook.com/leoniecheethamart

www.dinahmiller.com

To Al

Truth, love, and sacrifice.

.

BAD PENNY

Several years ago, there was a murder. A "bad penny" was killed by a "badder penny". This is their story.

The dark FBI SUV drove through the late night as its headlights illuminated the red-desert dirt road on the Navajo Indian Reservation.

The radio broadcaster announced the latest headlines from the *Indian Times*: He said, "In the news today, forty-five methamphetamine traffickers were caught up in an interagency law-enforcement drug sweep across Arizona and New Mexico after thirteen teenagers died last month from a contaminated batch of crystal meth."

Thoroughly disgusted, the Navajo Nation Police Chief Samuel Bear leaned up to the left and turned off the radio. "Is it ever going to end?" He looked out into the night from the passenger's side of the SUV.

"No." The answer came swift from FBI Special Agent John Treehorn as his hands clenched the steering wheel in frustration.

"The Mesa Cartel has a grasp in this area that's difficult to break," Samuel stated the cause.

"You don't have to tell me. I know," replied the half-Navajo, serious agent.

"The poverty, the lack of hope, they crush our youth." Samuel sighed.

Treehorn stated in all seriousness, "With the number of crimes on the reservation, they should all go into law enforcement." Headlights came closer, then whisked past them.

"We're losing a whole generation to drugs," Samuel said. "Grandparents are raising our babies."

Another car whizzed by, then darkness again.

"The babies need to be taught drugs aren't their answer, only their demise." Treehorn knew prevention education was one aspect of their survival.

"My demise would have come sooner if I was in this vehicle a minute longer with Edy Sheffield," Samuel blurted out.

"I understand." He looked out at the long stretch of highway ahead of them. "Since when did a transporting a prisoner to Cibola Federal feel like we were the ones being punished?" Treehorn eyed his friend.

Samuel chuckled as he wiped his police uniform, "I feel like I could use a shower now."

Treehorn nodded in the darkness as if Samuel could see. "Prisoner Transport owes us one after that," Treehorn felt dirty, too.

"Was your recorder on the whole time?" asked the chief.

"Yes. I'll let you listen to it, again, when you feel you're not doing your job." The Fed offered.

Samuel swore he heard Treehorn chuckle.

The agent added what they both knew, "I hope whatever behind-closed-doors information he gave the courts was worth it, but I know we haven't seen the last of Eli."

3

"Prisoner number 85721 won't cause problems on the Rez for a few years." Samuel said, "That, at least, made it worthwhile."

"He's a member of Indian Posse. We'll run into another one of them real soon, that's a given."

Treehorn's thoughts turned inward reviewing what he knew about Indian Posse. They were a ruthless gang, led by Parker Greyhorse, who took justice into their own hands when a white man failed to pay their debt to society when a native became a victim of a crime on the Rez. The FBI and he personally had numerous confrontations with them over the years. Everyone thought *Leave No Witness* was their motto. The agent knew otherwise.

Treehorn slowed his speed on the dirt road as he neared Samuel's village. Crime here, on the land of his mother's people, impacted everyone. Sad cases of trying to dig out of the poverty and hopelessness weighed heavily on their minds. He glanced at the structures that dotted the drive. Many still lived without electricity or running water, as if society didn't care about their basic human needs. As the horizon lightened, Treehorn wondered what it would take for things to change. The only future jobs on the reservation, and no laughing matter, appeared to be in law enforcement, rehabilitation, and rural utilities.

The muzzle flash of a gun lit up a darkened window of a little clapboard house.

Treehorn slammed on the brakes and the SUV skidded on the gravel until it came to a dusty halt. The agent activated the vehicle's red and blue lights which alerted any occupants that the police had arrived on the scene.

"Who lives here?" Treehorn shouted as he exited the driver's side with his hand-held police radio and ran for cover behind the SUV.

Samuel grabbed their bullet-proof vests from the back seat and joined the agent at the rear of the vehicle.

"Beth Hopper," The men hurriedly dressed into their protective and labeled vests.

"Any criminal history?" The Fed asked as he pulled his pistol from its holster.

"None that I know of." Samuel typed information into his departmental phone, "No, nothing with NNP."

"Dispatch." Treehorn notified his command.

"Go ahead." The operator responded.

"FBI Special Agent John Treehorn with NNP Chief Samuel Bear. We have gunfire at 86 Saguaro Road. Send backup."

"10-4. Units en route."

Treehorn observed a motorcycle parked in the driveway under a single light bulb hung from a dilapidated shack. "How old is the kid?"

Samuel followed the agent's eye, "Not old enough to own that hog."

As Treehorn and Samuel approached the house, a second gun flash occurred inside, then silence. The eerie quiet made it feel like death had just paid a visit.

Treehorn pointed to the rear of the house.

Samuel raised his gun and ran.

The Fed shouted towards the house, "This is the FBI and Navajo Nation Police. Your house is surrounded."

Silence.

"Come out with your hands up, now!" Treehorn shouted.

An older woman's voice spoke from inside of inside the house, "We're coming out."

The grandmother looked at her last living direct offspring, "Don't say a word to the policeman and don't answer a single question. Give me your word on your parents' graves."

Her only grandchild, Mel, nodded.

"Let's go and keep your hands up where the police can see them."

"What about him?" the teenager pointed at the man who had two bullet holes in his chest.

"We don't touch dead bodies."

The porch light illuminated the front area as the elderly woman and kid exited the house with their hands raised. They stopped beneath the light, so the police would know they weren't threats and become the targets of a lawman's bullet.

The agent approached the light, "Who's inside?"

The pair of Indians eyed the officer, the gold shield on his belt, and his black revolver.

The grandmother answered, "One dead Indian Posse gang member."

Meanwhile, the short-haired kid evaded Treehorn's eyes and focused on the toes that peeked out from torn, dirty sneakers.

"Anyone else?"

"No one." she replied.

Samuel yelled from inside of the house, "All clear."

Treehorn didn't lower his weapon. "Any weapons or sharp items on you?"

The two Indians shook their heads.

Samuel stepped out. "Male DOA, gunshot victim."

"Keep your arms raised. Samuel, check their

pockets." Treehorn ordered as he kept his pistol aimed at the pair.

Samuel's uniform and name tag identified him as he conducted a pat down. "They're clean."

"Lower your arms." Treehorn holstered his weapon and moved closer to the woman, "I'm FBI Special Agent John Treehorn. What's your name?"

"I'm Beth Hopper, and this is my grandchild, Mel." Her frail, aged voice spoke.

"What happened?"

"Mel's underage and I'm the guardian. You don't have permission to ask any questions without me being present." The frailty disappeared.

"I simply asked you what happened," Treehorn stated.

"Did Mel shoot the man?" Samuel interrupted.

"We want a lawyer," Beth demanded.

"Which one of you am I arresting?" Treehorn countered.

Neither Indian answered, they just stared at Treehorn.

"Do you know who owns the weapon?"

Samuel asked.

Silence from the two, again.

Treehorn activated his police radio.

"This is Dispatch, go ahead."

"FBI Special Agent John Treehorn. Cancel en route patrols. NNP is assisting."

"10-4, Agent Treehorn."

Samuel watched as two of his deputies arrived.

Two Navajo Nation Police vehicles pulled into the driveway with their flashing lights and sirens. Dustin Tsosie, a late-twenties deputy stepped from his vehicle and an older deputy, Freddy Chee, exited the other.

Samuel motioned for his deputies to join the group.

"Dustin and Freddy, you know Special Agent John Treehorn."

The men acknowledged each other.

Treehorn removed his handcuffs and met the woman's eyes, "Place your hands in front of you, ma'am. We're taking you both in for questioning."

Samuel's eyebrows rose at Treehorn's maneuver. The agent never had handcuffed an elder. Young punks, yes. Little old ladies, never.

Treehorn's handcuffs snapped closed. The silver metal appeared foreign against her aged and frail bony hands. Treehorn turned her towards Samuel, "Connect her to the security rod in my vehicle and bring back my evidence kit. Dustin, would you watch her?"

The deputy nodded.

Samuel whispered in the elder's ear, "He's a good man, but you left him no choice."

The woman gave a little nod of silent understanding.

"Freddy, watch the perimeter," Samuel ordered as Dustin and he assisted the woman across the uneven dirt of her property.

Treehorn didn't speak but watched the teenager's eyes follow the elderly woman's old shoes shuffle across gravel. This showed the Fed all he needed to know about this case. "Do you have anything on you that the Police Chief missed?"

The kid removed a single coin from the jean's front, left pocket and handed it to Treehorn.

The agent examined both sides and placed it in his pocket for safe keeping.

Samuel returned with the crime-scene evidence kit and an extra pair of handcuffs which Treehorn used to secure the teenager.

"Your vehicle." Treehorn handed the young one off to Samuel.

The chief's face silently questioned Treehorn's tactics but the officer complied with the Fed's order, walked the kid to his vehicle, and secured the silent youngster inside.

The elder woman spoke to Deputy Tsosie as soon as Samuel arrived at the vehicle, "You're not to question my grandchild without me being present."

Dustin looked at his boss for confirmation, who nodded.

"Just keep an eye on them," Samuel ordered as he closed the SUV's doors.

The deputy nodded. "What happened inside?"

"An Indian Posse member met a couple bullets."

"Who's going to pay for that?" Deputy Tsosie asked.

"I'm sure one of us will." Samuel stated matter-of-factly and sadly the premonition came true.

Treehorn stepped inside of the small house with his kit in hand. He found an Indian sprawled on the floor with two gunshot wounds to his white t-shirt covered chest, one bloody, and the other not so much.

A mother-of-pearl handled revolver, inlaid with *DWJ,* rested on the floor next to the body. Treehorn pulled on a pair of vinyl gloves and worked the crime scene with numbered plastic triangles. He took images of the gun, the deceased, and his rear pocket where a chain connected to black leather.

The agent removed the wallet and stepped

away from the body. The New Mexico driver's license listed the details needed for the FBI. Treehorn first provided the dispatcher with his name and badge number, "One DOA gunshot victim: Theo Nez, no middle name. Date of birth: June 20, 1982. Navajo. Address 3021 Kingman Road, Gallup. Send an agent out. Send the coroner to 86 Saguaro Road, CSU, and notify Agent Raven Shelly."

"Yes, sir. Agent Shelly reported in earlier when he heard the report over the NNP radio. He's already en route to your location."

"Thank you. Treehorn out."

Samuel entered and eyed the body. "Do we have an ID?"

"Navajo, Theo Nez."

"He looks familiar to me," Samuel said.

"Yes, he does." Treehorn looked around the small house. "Raven's on his way. I'll do a quick check and then I'll transport her."

Samuel wanted to say something, but wisdom held his thoughts and he kept his mouth closed.

Treehorn examined the neat, clean kitchen. The child's room was in the same condition. The grandmother's room provided a history of her family. Pictures of a younger couple graced the walls. There was a wedding picture, a single birth announcement, and then twin obituaries. Their deaths were caused by a tragic, late-night, motor vehicle accident.

Beth's room held an overloaded bookshelf with holistic medicine, spiritual guidance, and the latest crime thrillers. He placed a triangle on her nightstand and took a picture of her medications, bagged them, and placed a few clothing items into a brown paper bag.

The sun rose over the horizon as Agent Raven Shelly arrived on site. Two years younger than his fellow agent and still working towards his Special Agent status, Treehorn knew Raven would provide any backup needed for this investigation.

"How did the two of you end up here?" Raven handed coffee's to the officers.

"We were returning from Cibola when we came upon the shooting in progress," Treehorn answered.

Samuel joked to Raven, "Do you sleep with the police radio?"

"No. Sick kid. Dana took over, so I could leave. So, what happened?" Raven's investigative mind kicked in.

"Indian Posse member, Theo Nez. DOA with two bullet holes to the chest. One fancy, initial inlaid gun, two suspects and neither one is talking."

Raven looked at the suspects as they waited in the separate vehicles illuminated by the interior dimmer light and the early morning sunshine.

Two more NN police cruisers arrived, their blue-and-red lights highlighted the area.

"Samuel, will you transport Mel Hopper?"

The police chief nodded to Treehorn.

"I'd like your deputies to stay for backup in case any Indian Posse members have a notion to cause problems as the coroner removes the body."

"Raven, you're in charge and check the

16

motorcycle too." Treehorn ordered, "I'll have these two processed for interrogation. Return to the office when CSU is finished."

Samuels's phone beeped, and he read the screen.

"There was a report filed yesterday morning that my officers pursued Theo Nez, near here, for speeding and suspicious activity. A drug deal went down a few blocks away. Police swarmed the area."

"Did they speak to him?" The Fed asked.

"No, he eluded the officers,"

"That's a strange coincidence for Theo to have been in this area when he lives in Gallup," Treehorn surmised.

Raven and Samuel looked at each other and concluded the same.

Treehorn never believed in coincidences.

The Special Agent climbed into his SUV and set the brown paper bag on the passenger seat. He looked at the woman in his rear-view mirror. "I brought your medications and some clothes for you."

Beth remained silent.

"I don't want to see Mel go to prison,"

She met Treehorn's eyes in the rearview mirror, "I have nothing to say to you."

"How long has Indian Posse been visiting?"

Beth's eyes turned away and refused to speak for the duration of the trip.

Treehorn and Samuel transported the suspects to the FBI office in Gallup and, upon their arrival, kept the two Indians separated at all times. They were tested for gunshot residue and fingerprinted. Techs collected their clothing as evidence and it was forwarded, along with the other samples, to the forensic lab for analysis. Each had to put on a dehumanizing orange jumpsuit.

Treehorn went to Raven's office and continued his investigation. Theo Nez's criminal record held two felony drug convictions, one in

Tucson, Arizona and one in Brownsville, Texas. Treehorn opened the email sent by Samuel with the summary of the NNP chase. Three-strike laws would have given Theo a solid reason to evade the deputies, but what business did he have with Beth or Mel? Neither of them had any criminal history or activity.

Dr. D. Gallagher telephoned the Agent with his no-nonsense preliminary. "COD was the first bullet to the heart. The second bullet was for show. Meaning, he was already dead when the second bullet hit him. His urine did test positive for drugs, and he had been in a recent fight. One cracked rib with abdominal bruises. You'll get a copy of the final results."

"Thanks, Doc."

Su Hawkins, a CSU, telephoned Treehorn next with the short-ballistics preliminary report. "Two sets of fingerprints were on the gun, including the trigger. You've got them both in custody. I can't tell you a hundred percent which one fired the kill shot because either one could have pulled the trigger."

"Who owns the gun?" The agent asked.

"I don't know, Treehorn, something isn't right. I submitted images of the gun, its description, each bullet's lands and grooves, and its rifling into my computer. An ATF warning appeared, "Higher Security Clearance Required". I've never seen that."

"Send everything you have completed to my phone: detailed images of the revolver, images of the bullets rifling, fingerprints, and whatever else you've noted, okay?"

"Will do," Su whispered.

"Su. ATF will be showing up shortly. Don't transfer anything over to them until you get a copy of their identification and their signatures. Hide everything. I'll back you up."

"Thanks, Treehorn."

Less than a minute later, the agent's telephone beeped several times in succession as the files arrived. He then forwarded everything he received from his tech to his encrypted, secure server.

Treehorn received the last phone call he needed from the CSU, Elizabeth Barney. "All I have is the preliminary. Both sets of clothing tested positive for blood and gunshot residue. Both Beth and Mel Hopper were standing next to each other when the gun fired and killed Theo Nez. I'll be sending every item to Quantico for further testing."

"ATF will be coming for the gun. It flagged as a high-security alert. Send those reports to my phone and secure the clothing. When ATF shows up and asks you to surrender the items, refuse and call me. Then, I'll handle it."

"Will do. Thanks for the heads up, Treehorn." Elizabeth hung up.

The agent added Elizabeth's messages to his server. He reviewed each message. As soon as he received verification that they were uploaded securely, he deleted all of the CSU and ballistic data from his phone.

At this point, Treehorn knew two things: Beth and Mel held the answers to the death of Theo Nez, and the FBI ballistics lab possessed a gun that was part of a larger, federal investigation.

Raven greeted Treehorn when he returned to the office, "Nothing unexpected turned up during the sweep."

He nodded, not surprised. The agent updated his co-worker on the latest forensics results including the security alert set into motion by the revolver. He grabbed a medical item, "I need your help."

Treehorn and Raven stopped first and looked into Mel's interrogation room. The teen's orange-suited back faced the door as the kid looked out the steel-barred window and refused to acknowledge their presence.

The agent eyed the gray-haired, older guard who was a father of five. "Monette," nodding toward the suspect, "has Mel said anything?"

"Not a single word. Just watches freedom through the window. Look where it got the kid, not having a father figure." Monette blamed everything on the breakdown of family values.

"Let me know if anything changes."

Treehorn whispered to Raven, "Guard the door," as they walked towards Beth's holding cell.

"Hey, Timothy." The agents observed the poor sap who repeatedly and routinely worked guard duty. His focus appeared more directed at his novel than toward the little old lady in the room.

"Treehorn, Raven." The paperback disappeared.

"What did you do this time?" Raven asked.

The agent whispered, "Bestseller came out yesterday, so I volunteered." Timothy patted his pocket.

"Go take a break," Treehorn ordered.

Timothy looked at his two co-workers who nodded in the direction of the break room. He understood. "How long?"

"Fifteen."

Timothy nodded and whistled as he walked away, removing the book out of his pocket.

Raven stood watch as Treehorn entered the interrogation room.

Beth saw his reflection in the secured window as she gazed outside. She made no comment.

Treehorn placed an item on the table and slammed his palm against it. "Have a seat. I have a couple of questions to ask."

Beth fidgeted in the uncomfortable chair as Treehorn handed her an ice pack. "Do you want to have that examined by a doctor?"

"No." The frail hand placed the treatment against her swollen and bruised face.

"Who hit you?" he questioned.

No response.

"You know, Mel has the same view as you."

She didn't respond.

"Did you receive your medications?"

Beth nodded.

"You can change your clothing when you wish. I brought your items. I know you're aware of that. I told you before."

"Thanks."

"Do you wish to have an attorney present?"

"Am I being arrested?" Beth countered.

"Not this minute, Mrs. Hopper, but I do have the preliminary results and they show the blood spatter, the gunshot residue, and fingerprints on the gun." He watched her and continued, "I'm sure this doesn't surprise you since you both were standing side by side when the gun fired." He wished for a response.

Silence.

"I'm going to turn this over to the Federal District Attorney's Office. I know, one of you killed Theo Nez and that makes the other an accessory."

Beth's old eyes held onto the truth, "Go tell Parker Greyhorse I have ten kilos of Indian Posse's drugs. Theo dropped them off to Mel when he spotted the Navajo Police in the area. Tell Greyhorse that if he wants them back, he'll make a deal with the D.A. for Mel and me."

Treehorn stood up. Anger emanated from him. These kids didn't stand a chance on the reservation and now an elder controlled his investigation.

Raven whistled patiently as he guarded the interrogation room. Two fellow agents, Cortez and Rivera, tried to peek into the door's window.

Raven successfully stepped in front of them and blocked their view.

"Who's interviewing?"

"Treehorn and do not disturb him, if you know what's good for you."

The two agents eyed each other, and Cortez voiced what Rivera thought, "The kid did it. Why's Treehorn wasting his time on a little old lady?"

All three agents snapped to attention as the door unexpectedly opened. They moved back as Treehorn stormed by them without commenting.

"What a prick!" whispered Rivera, the newest agent in Gallup.

Raven chuckled at the pair, "You haven't a clue."

Cortez yelled at Treehorn, "Are you arresting the kid?"

"I'm going to see Parker Greyhorse," Treehorn answered.

Raven's smile disappeared, "Alone?" He shouted.

Treehorn offered no comment to the men as he strode away.

"Why would he visit Greyhorse without backup?" Rivera questioned.

Raven asked himself the same question but didn't voice it to the junior officers.

BAR NONE, an Indian Posse establishment.

No one really knows how long Indian Posse held the building as their clubhouse, but the Feds routinely raided it anytime a member held an outstanding warrant. This allowed law enforcement a reason for a legal search. It netted a few men here and there, but never any drugs. Parker Greyhorse, the leader of Indian Posse, made sure the rules established long ago continued to be followed. Any man who committed an infraction paid a hefty price.

Treehorn exited his vehicle without his suit jacket. His crisp white shirt contrasted with his dark tan, black hair, gold badge, and the leather holster that held his pistol. His long legs strode toward the entrance where the muscular, thirty-year-old bouncer, Ike Johnson, made the mistake of raising his hand to block Treehorn from entering their establishment.

The surprise showed in the whites of Ike's eyes as the agent's fist flew at and smashed into the man's face. The blinding pain doubled him over as he clutched his blood-gushing nose.

Treehorn took a measured step back as the bouncer straightened.

Ike couldn't have foreseen the agent's size-thirteen shoe would impact his chest with such force that it would knock his body backward and cause it to crash through the clubhouse entrance. The bouncer landed perfectly at the feet of his boss, Parker Greyhorse, who sat drinking his beer at the saloon-style bar.

Ike struggled to stand. His broken rib

competed with his broken nose for a pain competition.

"You always could make an entrance, Treehorn," Parker stated. He glanced at Ike as the Indian Posse members formed a perimeter around the three men.

Ike remained down. He didn't want to go another round with the Fed nor did he want the wrath of his boss.

Parker's toe tapped the injured man's head, "Get your ass to the healer and consider yourself lucky, today."

Both Treehorn and Parker participated in a staring contest and ignored the injured man as he struggled to stand.

No one offered a helping hand to the shamed bouncer as he found his footing and limped away.

Parker lifted one index finger and motioned for his men to back off.

They returned to their respective seats and maintained their sights on Greyhorse and Treehorn.

The Fed privately noted their identities and the loyalty they exhibited to the Posse leader.

Parker nudged a bar stool toward the agent with his cowboy boot.

Treehorn took the seat as Parker motioned to the bartender for a round of drinks.

Neither man spoke again until the barmaid placed two napkins down, a cold beer atop one for Parker and a bottled water for the Special Agent.

"Hello, Treehorn," the bartender greeted him.

"Hi, Nola, how's the family?"

"Everyone's good." She glanced down at Treehorn's napkin. "Enjoy your drinks."

Both men waited for her to walk away before resuming their conversation.

"What brings you here, Treehorn?"

"Theo Nez."

Parker waited. Nothing was secret on the Rez.

"Two bullets to the chest."

"That's a crying shame. We had a little run-in with him, recently."

"Care to elaborate?" Treehorn grilled.

"We heard that he was dealing on the side."

"What side was that?"

"The side we don't allow." Parker took a drink from his longneck.

"I have the ten kilos..." Treehorn paused intentionally and observed no reaction from Parker, "...and the gun." Treehorn witnessed Parker's fingers tighten on the bottle at the mention of the weapon.

The Indian Posse leader paused before speaking. "He lost his membership when we confronted him about the narcotics."

Treehorn waited.

Parker pursed his lips and chose his words with extreme care, "Theo told us that the money for the drug deal came with an understanding that the gun in question would be returned to its rightful owner. How he came to acquire it, we never asked."

Treehorn glanced at the INDIAN POSSE display board attached to the wall and labeled *Bad Penny* at its top. One empty spot, dead center, stood out. Upon closer inspection, several empty slots

31

lined the perimeter.

Parker followed Treehorn's attention, "Did you find anything useful on his body?"

"Not a single thing," Treehorn answered as he finished his water, dropped a tip, and pocketed the napkin.

Every Posse member watched as Treehorn walked to the *Bad Penny* display and fulfilled his need to touch the penniless slot in the center. No one commented as he turned and walked out.

He unfolded the napkin as he sat in his vehicle and read the single word hastily written on it. It spelled, "Shipley".

Treehorn's telephone beeped with a message from the local supervisor, "My office, now!"

He parked his vehicle next to the ATF-marked vehicle. He glanced at the license plate to see who received the orders, then walked straight to FBI District Supervisor Eli Henderson's office. The agent knocked once and entered.

Henderson sat patiently behind his clutter-free desk. Bureau of Alcohol, Tobacco, Firearms, and Explosives Associate Deputy Director Colin Finch waited in one chair while Federal District Attorney Susie Shipley sat in the other.

Everyone knew everyone, so preliminaries were bypassed as Treehorn stood at attention in his natural poise.

"Your lackey refused to turn the gun over to us." Finch didn't look happy.

"We have a dead Indian Posse member shot with that revolver." Treehorn reiterated for the prosecutor knowing that everyone would have already been briefed on the murder.

"Our investigation takes precedence," Finch demanded.

Treehorn casually leaned against the wall. "What case is that?"

No one answered the simple question.

"Turn the gun over, Treehorn." Eli Henderson ordered his subordinate.

The agent removed his phone and dialed CSU Su Hawkins, "ATF Finch will be appearing at your door shortly. Make sure he presents his identification, signs his name, and prints his name on the transfer order for the gun. Then send me a copy of paperwork before he takes possession of the weapon and Su, make sure every "t" is crossed and every "i" is dotted."

Finch stood in anger, "You half-breed prick!"

"Hey!" Henderson shouted.

Treehorn didn't move a hair as his eyes met Finch's but the corner of his mouth rose slightly.

The movement fueled Finch's anger as he stormed out and slammed the door in his wake.

"Take a seat, Treehorn," Henderson ordered.

The agent casually sat in Finch's warm seat. No one commented on the ATF's lack of professionalism. It was as if they all had heard the same song and dance before.

Henderson added, "That man must hold a lot of other people's skeletons in his closet to be able to keep his job."

Shipley, who had a long history in dealing with the angry Finch, caustically commented, "I think they're trying to escape."

Treehorn knew everyone held secrets and remained silent.

Shipley started, "I received two interesting calls prior to my arrival here. Do you gentlemen want to know from whom?"

Neither Fed speculated. Sometimes, it was best to keep one's mouth shut.

"DEA Quintero and Parker Greyhorse."

The agents looked at each other.

She continued, "The DEA informed me that a known drug supplier and known associate of Theo Nez turned up dead early this morning. Ten kilos of pure white heroin are missing. Parker Greyhorse told me that you and Beth Hopper know where they may be located, Agent Treehorn. I guess he doesn't want our eyes on him or his enterprise."

"Indian Posse doesn't deal in narcotics," Treehorn uttered the one indisputable fact in this case.

"I know, but here we are with Mr. Greyhorse providing crucial information about the drugs."

"I..." Henderson started but stopped when Shipley's hand rose.

"Interesting thing, the DEA and Indian Posse both provided me with the drug trafficker's name, an Ethan Bridges. I wondered if they worked together to bring the deal down."

"I..." Henderson attempted to speak again, stopped again from Shipley's raised hand.

The District Attorney's eyes focused on Treehorn, "You don't have a gun for a murder case. Your two suspects are going to wait for years to have their case tried. Deliver the heroin to the DEA, so it's off the streets. Hand me a written confession, and I'll support a suitable sentence." Shipley provided an option.

The agent thought, "That's easier said than done."

Treehorn was informed as soon as he left

Henderson's office that Beth's church members had requested to speak to him in the conference room.

When the agent entered, he found them waiting with Mary Sweetwater, his office coordinator. She had taken the day off to gather the members together, so they could speak to him.

Treehorn listened to each of them.

They spoke of Beth's love for her community. They spoke of the deeds she had done to help the elders on the reservation. All the while, they explained how she had suffered a grief that no parent should ever have to experience. She had buried her only son and his wife, then moved forward by giving everything she had to raising her only grandchild, her last living relative, Mel.

Mary gave Treehorn a supportive hug and voiced the last sentiment as the church group walked away, "She raised and protected Mel since the tragedy. Beth will tell you the truth. Treat her with the dignity she deserves, and she'll respect you for it."

Raven watched as they quietly departed. "They won't give up the other."

"I'll get a confession."

"How will you when neither one will talk?"

"The truth."

Treehorn turned off the audio recorder as he entered Beth's holding cell. Raven stood guard far enough away in case they needed something, but not close enough to hear their conversation.

Beth appeared pale and drawn. Even the colorful clothing she now wore brought no life to her dying spirit.

"I spoke with the Federal District Attorney Susie Shipley. She'll examine your written statement of the events and then make a suitable recommendation for sentencing."

The elder fidgeted in the chair and contemplated her life's choices.

Treehorn knelt at her feet, took her hand, and looked into her wise eyes, "Beth, the recorder is off. No one is within hearing. Please, tell me what happened that night. You're the only one that can make this right."

And, she did.

And, he listened.

She told him about the drugs, the threats, the violence, the deals, and the confrontation with the gun. The penny dropped.

Treehorn asked Beth one question.

She answered, "Yes."

He stood, exited the room, and typed up the report to be submitted to Shipley.

Raven saw the devastation on his friend and fellow agent's face. He didn't ask for the details.

Treehorn transported Beth and Mel home from their holding cells after Shipley read the statement and agreed to its stipulations.

Two Navajo Nation Police vehicles followed the agent.

Treehorn let the pair off at their front door for the night.

The two deputies hunkered down for their

overnight watch of the house-arrest prisoner.

Meanwhile, Treehorn recovered all ten kilos of the hidden heroin and turned them over to the DEA officer-in-charge who notified Shipley of the done deed.

In the morning, Treehorn and Raven arrived at the house. The agent grabbed the arrest warrant that he had pitched onto the dashboard earlier.

"I hate arresting teenagers," Raven stated as he reached for his door handle.

"I want you to stay outside," requested Treehorn.

Raven halted, surprised.

"I'll do this alone." Treehorn watched as Raven's eyebrows rose.

Raven didn't question his fellow agent's action, "I'll be here if you need me."

Treehorn nodded once.

Raven exited the SUV and watched as Treehorn approached the house. He would swear to his dying day that his friend staggered as he approached the front door, knocked, and then entered the home to perform his official duties.

Deputy Jimmy Begay, the house-arrest guarding officer approached Raven, "One-man show?"

"Agent Treehorn and I have this. You're relieved of your assigned duties."

The deputy shrugged and lifted his hand-held radio. He issued an order to his co-worker at the rear of the house, "Hey Janette, Feds are here. Agent Shelly says we can leave."

"10-4."

"Call us if you need us." Deputy Begay said sarcastically.

Raven watched as the NNP deputies drove away. A movement on the road caught his attention. Ten church members, including Mary Sweetwater, dressed in their ceremonial garb, came to Beth's house to offer their support in her time of need.

The members nodded solemnly to Raven as they passed him. They formed two lines from the front door of the old house to the FBI's black SUV. The church members chanted spiritual songs which would guide the family on their journey.

Raven listened to the beat of the drum, music he had grown up with since his childhood. These were songs about truth, love, and the sacrifice one made for one's family.

The door opened and Treehorn emerged from the cabin with one person in handcuffs.

Raven's eyes rounded in astonishment as Treehorn led Beth from the old homestead.

She looked neither left nor right but straight ahead at the vehicle that would remove her from the only home she'd ever known.

Treehorn allowed her to set the pace, for it was her time to go.

She stumbled slightly and Treehorn's strong arms helped her once again stand straight and tall.

The elders silence their song as she passed, supporting her, and finally honoring her by holding their fists across their hearts.

Mel emerged from the house and ran hysterically toward Beth.

The church elders turned their backs as the youth ran past them.

The teenager fell upon the red dirt, sobbing, "I'm sorry."

Beth didn't look back, even after Treehorn placed her inside the SUV.

The agent didn't look at Mel as he reached for his driver's door handle, but he hesitated when he looked at the elder as she sat stoically in the rear seat.

Raven watched the scene unfold as all the church elders walked away in silent judgment.

Beth's eyes stared straight ahead. Calm or resigned, the agent couldn't tell. She didn't move as Treehorn returned to the teenager.

He reached down and pulled Mel up by the shirt collar so they were looking eye to eye. His anger tightened his clenched fist as he shook the kid. "Do not dishonor your grandmother. Do you understand?"

The teenager nodded as tears mixed with the red-dusted cheeks.

Treehorn handed the kid his embroidered handkerchief to clean up. "You were given a choice today. You can crawl, or you can stand tall."

The youth nodded and used the handkerchief.

"You can make her proud or dishonor her. The choice is yours."

Wiping away the last tear, Mel stood for the grandmother who had sacrificed everything.

Treehorn handed over a business card then walked back to his vehicle.

Raven climbed into the SUV and watched as Treehorn glanced back one last time.

A hand, made into a fist, covered Mel's heart. The teenager made a promise right then.

Treehorn drove away. This time, he didn't look back.

Beth Hopper, Special Agent Treehorn, and Susie Shipley watched as Judge Rose Trembley read over the written confession and attached sheets of documentation.

Shipley added, "The district attorney accepts this plea deal, Your Honor, and supports the attached sentencing recommendation."

The judge read the documents, "Why do I question whether justice is being served, today?"

Beth spoke up, "I gave the confession willingly and honestly, Your Honor."

"I read the statements, Ms. Hopper, including a very detailed report from FBI Special Agent John Treehorn. I understand it, but do you understand the ramifications in their entirety?"

"I do, Your Honor."

"You don't have an attorney present, Ms. Hopper."

The elder woman spoke directly to the judge who understood Beth's words. "My consult was my church."

FBI Special Agent John Treehorn stood silent.

The judge took one long look at the grandmother, "I'll accept your guilty plea."

Beth asked the judge, "May I say one last thing?"

The judge nodded, Shipley listened, and Treehorn reflected as Beth spoke.

On the steps of the courthouse, an *Indian Times* journalist reported into his camera. "Today, Judge Rose Trembley accepted the guilty plea from seventy-four-year-old Beth Hopper for the shooting death of Theo Nez, an ex-Indian Posse gang member. Nez had allegedly entered Mrs. Hopper's house and threatened her family. Mr. Nez had a long rap sheet which included trafficking drugs to kids on reservations in both Arizona and New Mexico. The drugs originated from the Mesa Cartel, a vicious cartel in Sonora, Mexico. The DEA, assisted by the FBI, also removed ten kilos of pure white heroin from the streets which were associated with Mr. Nez's illegal drug trafficking.

Federal District Attorney Shipley added, "Beth Hopper was sentenced to two years for manslaughter and will serve those at the FCI facility in Tucson. She will be eligible for parole in twelve months, but it has been noted that Mrs. Hopper has been diagnosed with terminal, stage-four lung cancer. Hopper was allowed to address the court during her sentencing.

She stated, "The people have to stand up to the drug dealers that are killing our children and I would like to thank FBI Special Agent John Treehorn. Ms. Hopper refused to elaborate as to why she thanked the officer who arrested her." Shipley concluded with, "We consider this case closed and we'll have no further comment. May God have mercy on her soul."

BAR NONE

Treehorn stepped from his black FBI vehicle and buttoned up his suit jacket. His dark, conservative suit concealed his gun, badge, and handcuffs.

Ike Johnson stepped aside without a comment.

Treehorn walked inside and nodded to Nola as he sat down next to Parker Greyhorse, again.

She delivered a water to him and another beer for Parker.

"Well, if it isn't Mr. G-man or should I call you the Pennyman?"

Treehorn didn't respond. Instead, he slapped an embossed penny on the bar. It was the same penny Mel handed him the night of Theo Nez's death.

Greyhorse glanced at it and took a sip of his beer, "Name your poison."

"Mel Hopper is under my permanent protection."

Greyhorse's knuckles whitened around the beer bottle. "So be it. It's the Law of the Rez."

"Make sure Theo's half-brother, Bart, knows it too. In fact, make sure everyone knows it."

"I can't speak for him. He was disavowed

from Indian Posse when we kicked Theo out."

"Then, get the word to him in prison."

"I doubt he's going to survive the Texas prison."

"If by chance he does, then I'll deal with him when he's released." Treehorn finished his water. He examined the wall of pennies and each penny was labeled with a corresponding name. There were good ones and not so good ones.

Parker and Treehorn eyed the empty spot in the middle of the coins. They both knew what belonged there.

"Where's your penny?" Parker asked the agent.

Treehorn looked at his watch, the one his father gave him when he graduated from the FBI Academy, "The next time we meet, you'll be wearing my handcuffs."

"Do you want a make a bet on that?" Parker smiled.

Parker Greyhorse would lose that bet.

49

Beth Hopper died seven months later at FCI in Tucson. FBI Agent John Treehorn's vehicle led the funeral procession for the undertaker's vehicle from Tucson to the Navajo Indian Reservation. Her church members attended and paid their respects to her, not to her last grieving relative.

Two Years Later

Mel Hopper graduated from Window Rock High School. No one showed up to celebrate this achievement.

Four Years Later

Mel graduated from the University of Arizona. No one came to watch the student receive a criminal justice diploma.

Seventy-four Days Later

Seventy-four days later, out of respect for each of her grandmother's blessed years of life, Melanie "Mel" Hopper walked up the sidewalk to the FBI Academy in Quantico, Virginia.

Special Agent John Treehorn waited at the entrance.

"Hello, Treehorn." Melanie greeted him like a long-lost relative, handkerchief in hand.

"Hello, Grasshopper." Treehorn's greeting lacked any resemblance of affection.

A car passed the adults. Its speakers blared Nikka Costa's, *"Everybody got their something."*

Treehorn and Melanie eyes shifted from the music piper to each other.

Melanie smiled.

Treehorn didn't.

THE END

SHADOW DANCER A John Treehorn Mystery (Book 1) A dead man's clue sends FBI Special Agent John Treehorn to the Land of his People, the Navajo Indian Reservation, to hunt an elusive murderer named 'Shadow Dancer' the same Indian myth who brought this now decorated law enforcement officer to his knees. https://www.amazon.com/ebook/dp/B078RYVRC6

STOLEN SISTERS A John Treehorn Mystery (Book 2) FBI Special Agent John Treehorn hunts for a serial killer in an oil-field boomtown where several indigenous women have gone missing or murdered. https://www.amazon.com/ebook/dp/B07F1RYWKL

INDIAN POSSE A John Treehorn Mystery (Book 3) FBI Special Agent John Treehorn hunts for a killer on the Navajo Indian Reservation who murdered two members of Indian Posse, a ruthless gang that hunts criminals who have evaded the American justice system. Publication: January 2019.

Please join the author's page for future updates: www.facebook.com/SpecialAgentJohnTreehorn

Line Editor: Annie Darek

EBook formatted: https://www.word-2-kindle.com

www.dinahmiller.com

Made in United States
Orlando, FL
14 May 2023

33130209R00039